tHiS BOOK
BELONGS to:

_ _ _ _ _ _ _ _ _ _ _

_ _ _ _ _ _ _ _ _ _ _

31 Social Worker Coloring Pages

(Page 5-65)

10 Inspirational Quotes Coloring Pages

(Page 67-85)

Social Worker Coloring Pages

Social Worker Coloring Pages

18 Social Worker Coloring Pages

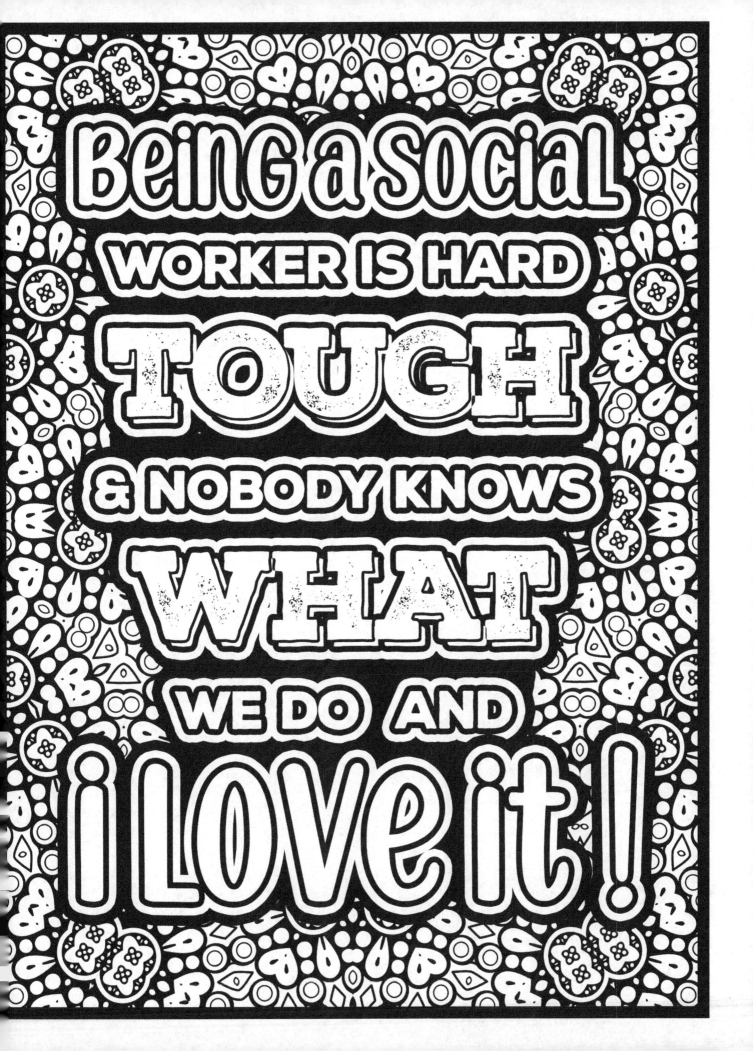

SOCIAL WORK MAKES ME HAPPY PAPERWORK NOT SO MUCH

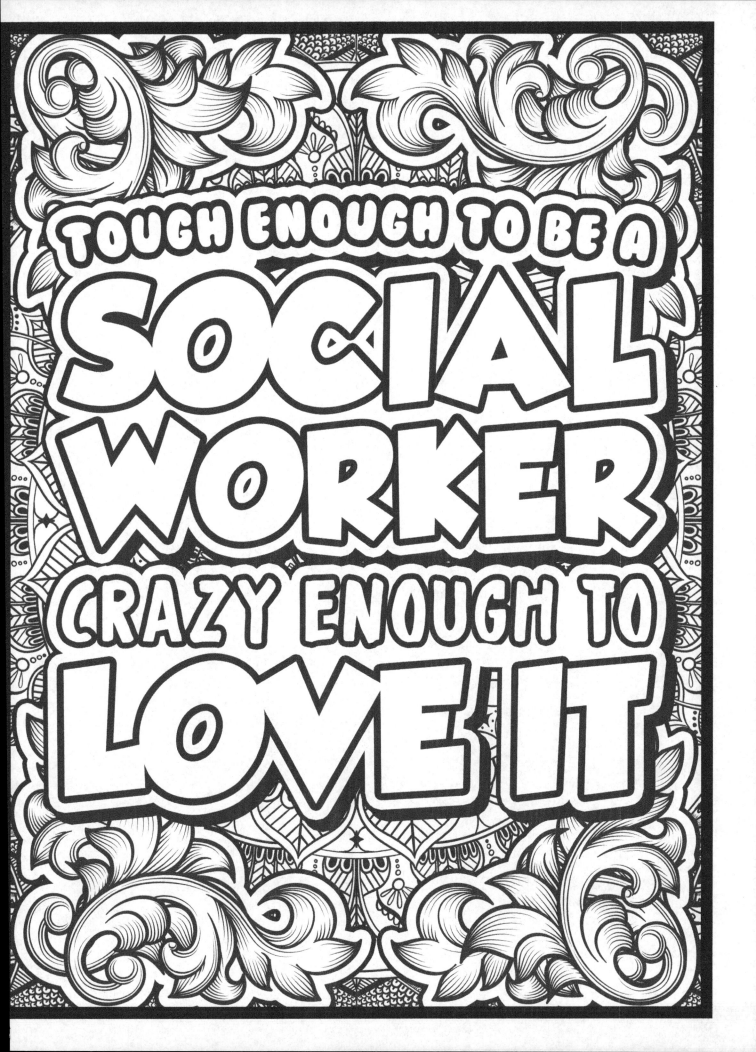

54 Social Worker Coloring Pages

Social Worker Coloring Pages

Inspirational Quotes Pages

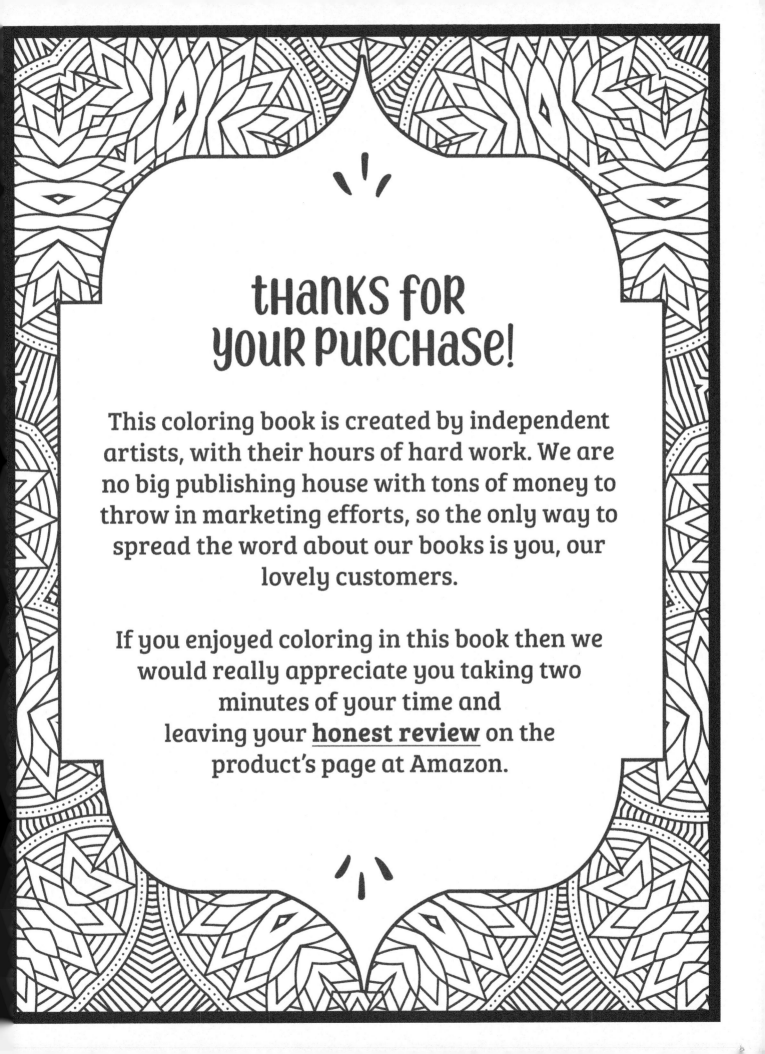

THANKS FOR YOUR PURCHASE!

This coloring book is created by independent artists, with their hours of hard work. We are no big publishing house with tons of money to throw in marketing efforts, so the only way to spread the word about our books is you, our lovely customers.

If you enjoyed coloring in this book then we would really appreciate you taking two minutes of your time and leaving your **honest review** on the product's page at Amazon.

Made in the USA
Coppell, TX
03 December 2024